THE
DISGUSTING
DICTIONARY

Compiled by Tracey Turner CRHW
(Collector of Rude and Horrid Words)

h

A division of Hodder Headline Limited

Introduction

Dictionaries are useful books but, unfortunately, the really interesting words are hidden among thousands of much duller ones. However, *The Disgusting Dictionary* only contains words that are fascinatingly horrible, rude or downright foul. In it you'll discover...

disgusting habits, including the posh word for picking your nose

how to be disgusting in a variety of foreign languages

85 ways to say 'vomit'

Elizabethan swear words

...and much more. Dip into this dictionary and you might encounter a gigantic dung-heap, fall down a long-drop toilet, sample some revolting food and meet a variety of disgusting creatures.

So read on for a feast of foulness...

Notes and Guide to Use...

The Disgusting Dictionary uses a rudeness rating system as follows:

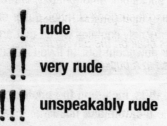

! rude

!! very rude

!!! unspeakably rude

It goes without saying that anything marked **!!!** should be used with extreme caution.

All words are identified as nouns, verbs or adjectives. For example:

crepitate (verb): to fart (literally, to make a crackling sound).

(An action word: He crepitated loudly.)

guano (noun): the poo of sea birds.

(A word used to name something: There is guano on the windscreen.)

4

mundungus (adjective): eighteenth-century word for foul smelling.

(A describing word: The dunny is mundungus.)

Some words can be used as both a verb *and* a noun. For example:

! boak (noun and verb): vomit (originally Scottish).

(Noun: There was boak on the pavement.)
(Verb: She boaked in a bucket.)

Please note that where a word also has other meanings which are not disgusting or rude, the other meanings are ignored. For example:

fruity (adjective): foul smelling, often applied to **air biscuits.**

Foreign words are given with no attempt at suggesting pronunciation.

You will find several examples of rhyming slang throughout the dictionary. These are words that rhyme with the word they stand for. The idea started in the East End of London so that people could disguise what they were really talking about. For example:

! Farmer Giles (noun): rhyming slang for **piles.**

Any tricky words or phrases have been put in **bold** for you to look up elsewhere in the dictionary.

abscess (noun): pus-filled swelling on or under the skin.

!! agent brown (noun): diarrhoea.

! air biscuit (noun): fart.

! air buffet (noun): stronger or more numerous version of **air biscuit**.

airhead (noun): idiot, a general insult.

! air muffin (noun): fart.

air the diced carrots (verb): to vomit.

! air tulip (noun): fart produced by someone very important or posh.

HIGH COURT

Allghoi Khorkhoi (noun): see Mongolian death worm.

!! anal announcement (noun): fart

!! anal salute (noun): fart.

anthropophagus (noun): posh word for **cannibal**.

apple-blossom two-step (noun): diarrhoea.

apple catchers (noun): really big knickers.

! apple tart (noun): fart (in Australian slang).

! aris (noun): bum (in rhyming slang:
aris = aristotle = bottle = bottle and glass = arse).

!! arse (noun): bum.

ass (noun): US version of arse.

Assassin bug (noun): insect
named after its disgusting habit of
ambushing other insects,
dissolving their body tissues with
deadly poison and then sucking
them up. Assassin bugs sometimes
eat one another, and also suck the
blood of humans, which can cause
the fatal **chagas disease**. These
insects are also known as kissing
bugs.

atomic wedgie (noun): extreme **wedgie**, where the aim
is to get the underpants over the head.

!! auditorium fart (noun): very loud and echoing fart.

Augean stables (noun): in Greek mythology, King Augeas's stables which contained 3,000 cattle and had not been cleaned for 30 years, resulting in an unimaginable quantity of **noisome ordure**. The task of cleaning them required superhuman strength and the hero Hercules only managed it by diverting the course of two rivers.

axillary hyperhidrosis (noun): posh word for unusually sweaty armpits.

Aztec two-step (noun): diarrhoea.

B

! back-door trots (noun): diarrhoea.

backside (noun): bum.

! backwards burp (noun): fart.

bacteria (noun): tiny single-celled organisms, which can cause disease and **putrefaction**.

disgusting fact

Bacteria in human poo can travel through ten layers of toilet paper.

! baff (noun): South African slang for fart.

bag of spanners (phrase): used to denote ugliness, 'you have a face like a bag of spanners' (see also box of frogs, bulldog chewing a wasp).

! bahookie (noun): Scottish slang for bum.

! bake an air muffin/air biscuit (verb): to fart.

baja ant (noun): see bullet ant.

bampot (noun): idiot, a general insult.

! barf (noun and verb): vomit.

! bark at ants (verb): to vomit.

!! bark carrots (verb): to vomit.

barn door is open, the (phrase): meaning 'your flies are undone'.

bás-iná (noun and verb): Romanian word for fart.

! bat-in-a-cave (noun): clearly visible bogey dangling in a nostril.

Baykok (noun): ghostly, skeletal creature with glowing red eyes. North American Indians fear the Baykok as they believe he kills people using invisible arrows.

beakie (noun): Scottish word for bodily gunge, such as the sticky bits found in the corners of eyes or between toes.

bean jacks (noun): Irish word for ladies' toilets.

bedbug (noun): small, reddish-brown insect found in bedding all over the world. These parasites come out at night to feast on human blood.

bedpan (noun): pan kept in the bedroom and used as a toilet (also known as chamber pot).

behind (noun): bum.

belch (noun and verb): to bring up wind from the stomach via the mouth (also known as burp).

biffy (noun): Canadian word for toilet.

bile (noun): thick greenish liquid stored in the gall bladder and used to help digestion. Sometimes makes an appearance after an extreme bout of **barking carrots**.

billitting (noun): scientific word for fox poo.

birdbrain (noun): idiot, a general insult.

bird's nest soup (noun): Chinese soup made from the nest of a type of swallow. The soup takes its special taste from the sticky saliva-like substance which the bird produces to hold its nest together.

black death (noun): the name given to the outbreak of bubonic plague in the fourteenth century, caused by rat

fleas. Symptoms included inflamed lymph nodes (or 'buboes'), high fever, headaches, vomiting and black spots on the skin. The disease killed one third of the population of Europe.

blackhead (noun): skin pore clogged with **sebum** (also known as comedo).

black pudding (noun): savoury pudding made from animal blood, common in the north of England (also known as blood pudding).

blähung (noun): German word for flatulence.

! blaps, the (noun): diarrhoea.

! blatts, the (noun): diarrhoea.

blockhead (noun): idiot, a general insult.

blood fluke (noun): highly dangerous parasitic worm.

blood pudding (noun): see black pudding.

!! **blow beets** (verb): to vomit.

!! **blow breakfast** (verb): to vomit.

!! **blow chow** (verb): to vomit.

disgusting fact

Lazzaro Spollanzani was an 18th century scientist with an interest in **chunder**. One of his experiments involved being sick then eating the puke, **ralphing** again and eating the puked puke, then **boaking** a third time and eating the puked puked puke.

!! **blow chunks** (verb): to vomit.

!! **blow (one's) cookies/lunch** (verb): to vomit.

‼ blow foam (verb): to vomit.

❗ blow off (noun and verb): fart.

blow raspberries (verb): to make a farting noise (see also raspberry tart).

‼‼ blow snot rockets (verb): to block one nostril while blowing strongly down the other — without using a handkerchief (see also bushman's hanky).

bludger (noun): Australian word for a lazy, useless person.

bluebottle (noun): large fly with blue body which lays its eggs in rotting meat or open wounds, also known as a blowfly.

blue-ringed octopus (noun): small octopus found off the coasts of Australia, New Guinea and the Philippines. Its bite is painless but can kill a human in minutes.

bluey (noun): Australian word for bluebottle jellyfish (see also Portuguese man-of-war).

! boak (noun and verb): vomit (originally Scottish).

bodewash (noun): scientific term for cow dung.

body odour (noun): disgusting smell of stale sweat on an unwashed human body, often shortened to B.O.

! bog (noun): toilet.

boga (noun): Urdu word for snot.

bogey (noun): hardened snot, sometimes forming a bat-in-a-cave.

boggin' (adjective): disgusting (originally Scottish).

! bog house (noun): toilet.

boil (noun): pus-filled swelling on skin.

!! Bondi cigar (noun): floating poo discovered while swimming in the sea (derived from Bondi beach in Australia), also known as brown-eyed mullet.

bonehead (noun): idiot, a general insult.

! booger (noun): US word for bogey.

bottom (noun): bum.

! bottom bassoon (noun): fart.

! bottom blast (noun): fart.

! bottom burp (noun): fart.

! bottom trumpet (noun): fart.

! bowff (noun and verb): Scottish word for vomit.

bowffin' (adjective): Scottish word for disgusting.

box jellyfish (noun): a type of jellyfish (see also sea wasp).

box of frogs (phrase): used to denote ugliness, from the phrase 'you have a face like a box of frogs' (see also bulldog chewing a wasp, bag of spanners).

bozo (noun): idiot, a general insult (from Bozo the Clown – a famous cartoon clown from the 1950s and 60s).

brawn (noun): jelly-like substance produced by boiling animal heads, eaten in many parts of Europe including Britain (also known as head cheese).

break wind (verb): to fart.

broekhoesten (verb): Dutch word for fart (literally meaning 'to cough in one's pants').

bromhidrosis (noun): posh word for body odour.

‼ brown-eyed mullet (noun): floating poo discovered while swimming in the sea (see also Bondi cigar).

‼ brown trout (noun): poo.

bubonic plague (noun): disease carried by rat fleas. Symptoms include inflamed lymph nodes (or 'buboes'), high fever, headaches, vomiting and black spots on the skin (also known as black death).

‼ bucket of snots (noun): Irish slang for ugly person.

bufflehead (noun): seventeenth-century word meaning idiot, a general insult.

builder's bum (noun): the display of the top part of someone's bum while bending over, usually seen on a building site (also known as builder's crevice).

builder's crevice (noun): see builder's bum.

!! bulldog chewing a wasp (phrase): used to denote ugliness, from the phrase 'you have a face like a bulldog chewing a wasp' (see also bag of spanners, box of frogs).

bullet ant (noun): ant found in parts of Central and South America. Its sting causes excruciating pain, which has been compared to the pain of being hit by a bullet, and lasts for up to five hours. Multiple stings can kill a human (also known as bala ant).

! bum (noun): the buttocks (also known as aris, arse, backside, bahookie, behind, bottom, butt, date, fundament, hind quarters, jacksie, keister, parking place, posterior, rear, rear end, rump, sit-me-down, sit-upon, sitting room, tail, toosh, tooshie, wazzoo).

! bum-face (noun): general insult.

! bum fodder (noun): toilet paper.

!!! bum gravy (noun): diarrhoea.

burp (noun and verb): to bring up wind from the stomach via the mouth (also known as belch).

!! burp borscht (verb): to vomit.

!! bushman's hanky (noun): Australian slang for **blowing snot rockets**.

bush oyster (noun): Australian slang for snot.

! butt (noun): US version of bum.

!! butt burp (noun): fart.

disgusting fact

Most people **parp** between 15 and 20 times a day. An adult man's daily production of bottom gas is roughly 600 ml.

‼ buttlick (noun): annoying person, a general insult (also known as buttmunch).

‼ buttly (adjective): very ugly (in US slang), a combination of 'butt' and 'ugly'.

‼ buttmunch (noun): see buttlick.

‼ buttock bassoon (noun): very loud fart.

buttons (noun): posh word for sheep poo.

! butt trumpet (noun): fart.

caca (noun): French and Spanish word for poo.

cacaca (noun): Portuguese word for poo (also known as coco).

cacca (noun): Italian word for poo.

! cack (noun): poo or rubbish.

! caffler (noun): Irish word for idiot, a general insult.

! call Hughy (verb): to vomit.

call the moose: see rôpe pa elgen.

can (noun): US word for toilet.

candlestick (noun): trail of snot running out of someone's nostril.

cannibal (noun): someone who eats human flesh (see also anthropophagus).

canopic jar (noun): jar in which Ancient Egyptians kept the entrails of dead bodies which had been mummified.

carbuncle (noun): large spot or boil.

carrion (noun): rotting dead flesh (or body) of an animal.

cesspit (noun): container for sewage (also known as cesspool).

cesspool (noun): see cesspit.

chagas disease (noun): disease caused by assassin bugs which, in extreme cases, causes swelling, vomiting, fever, heart problems and death.

chamber pot (noun): pot kept in the bedroom and used as a toilet (also known as bed pan, close stool, commode, gazunder, potty, rogue with one ear, thundermug, thunderpot).

cheese on your chin (phrase): Irish slang meaning 'your flies are undone'.

cheey-cheey (noun): Urdu word for urine (also known as shoo-shoo).

!! **chew the cheese** (verb): to vomit.

chiasse (noun): French word for diarrhoea.

chi-chi (noun): Hindi word for poo.

chiotte (noun): French word for toilet.

chitterlings (noun): pig
intestines stewed, then battered
and fried, and eaten in the
American South.

chorb (noun): South African word for spot.

chuck up (verb): to vomit.

! chunder (noun and verb): vomit.

!! chunderspew (noun and verb): vomit.

!! chunk (verb): to vomit.

!! chunk one's cookies/lunch (verb): to vomit.

chupacabra (noun): monster with long fangs, a spiked spine and glowing eyes said to kill small animals in Central and South America (literally means 'goat sucker').

! church fart (noun): silent fart (also known as fice, foist).

chyme (noun): ground-up food found in the intestine.

clackdish (noun): Elizabethan insult.

clarty (adjective): dirty.

cloaca (noun): Latin word for sewer (see also cloakroom).

cloakroom (noun): posh word for downstairs toilet, derived from **cloaca**.

close-stool (noun): seat with a **chamber pot** in it, an early version of the **commode**.

closet of ease (noun): nineteenth-century word for toilet.

clot (noun): fool, a general insult.

clotpole (noun): Elizabethan insult.

cludgie (noun): toilet.

cockroach (noun): disgusting insect that infests houses, spreads disease and is almost impossible to kill.

disgusting fact

A cockroach can live
for up to a week
without its head.

coco (noun): Portuguese word for poo (also known as cacaca).

comedo (noun): skin pore clogged with **sebum** (also known as blackhead).

comfort station (noun): nineteenth-century word for toilet.

commode (noun): seat with built-in **chamber pot**.

constipation (noun): inability to pass **faeces**.

coprolite (noun): fossilised dung.

coprology (noun): the study of poo (also known as scatology).

coprophagist (noun): dung-eater.

corpse flower (noun): plant found in Indonesia that smells of rotting flesh to attract insects and is the smelliest plant on earth (also known as **Titan Arum**).

coryza (noun): posh word for runny nose.

country pancake (noun): cow pat (also know as cow pie).

cow pie (noun): see also country pancake.

coyote ugly (adjective): very ugly indeed.

! crack (verb): to fart.

cradle cap (noun): oily, yellow and sometimes crusty dandruff often found on young babies.

! crap (noun and verb): poo.

Crimson rambler

crappy (adjective): rubbish, poor quality.

creep (noun): annoying or unpleasant person, a general insult.

crepitate (verb): to fart (literally, to make a crackling sound).

cries and screeches (noun): Australian rhyming slang for leeches.

crimson rambler (noun): nineteenth-century slang for bedbug (also known as tom tug).

disgusting fact

Cows make **country pancakes** an average of 16 times a day.

crotiles (noun): posh word for the poo of hares.

crubeen (noun): dish consisting of a pig's hind feet (see also pig's trotters).

crud (noun): something dirty or disgusting.

cruddy (adjective): disgusting, **grody**.

!! crud-sucking (adjective): absolutely disgusting.

cul (noun): French word for bum.

culo (noun): Spanish word for bum.

!! curl and hurl (verb): to vomit.

curl paper (noun): nineteenth-century word for toilet paper.

cuspidor (noun): container for spitting into (also known as spittoon).

‼ **cut a muffin** (verb): to fart.

‼ **cut a stinker** (verb): to fart.

‼ **cut the cheese** (verb): to fart (US slang).

dander (noun): animal dandruff.

dandruff (noun): flakes of dead skin, dirt and oil from the scalp (also known as **seborrheic dermatitis**).

date (noun): Australian slang for bum.

deadhead (noun): fool, a general insult.

! decorate the pavement (verb): to vomit.

defecate (verb): posh word meaning to poo.

! Delhi belly (noun): diarrhoea (particularly when on holiday abroad).

!! deliver pavement pizza (verb): to vomit.

!! depth charge (noun): underwater fart.

! diarrhoea (noun): liquid poo (see also agent brown, apple-blossom two-step, Aztec two-step, back-door trots, blaps, blatts, bum gravy, Delhi belly, jerry-go-nimble, Montezuma's revenge, Patagonian pasodoble, Rangoon runs, red hots, runny tummy, runs, rusty water, scitte, scutters, skitters, sour-apple quickstep, squirt, squirts, squits, squitters, trots, trouser chilli, wildies).

dill (noun): Australian slang for idiot, a general insult.

dimwit (noun): idiot, a general insult.

! dirt surfer (noun): an especially dirty or unhygienic person (also known as soap dodger).

disembowel (verb): to remove human or animal **entrails**.

disgorge (verb): to vomit.

do-a-cat (verb): nineteenth-century slang meaning to vomit.

! dog breath (noun): general insult.

dog's breakfast (noun): complete mess (also known as dog's dinner).

dolt (noun): fool, a general insult.

don't-mention-'ems (noun): nineteenth-century word for trousers.

D
Drongo

doo-doo (noun): poo.

! dook (noun): poo.

dork (noun): idiot, a general insult.

dreck (noun): dirt or rubbish.

dribble (noun and verb): to let saliva run from the mouth (see also slaver, drool).

drisheen (noun): Irish sausage made from sheep's blood.

!! drive the porcelain bus (verb): to vomit.

drongo (noun): Australian term for annoying person, a general insult.

drool (noun and verb): to let saliva run from the mouth (also known as dribble).

‼ drop one's guts (verb): to fart.

droppings (noun): poo.

dross (noun): rubbish.

duffis/duffus (noun): idiot, a general insult.

dump (noun and verb): poo.

dunderhead (noun): idiot, a general insult.

dung (noun): animal poo used to fertilise land (also known as manure).

dung beetle (noun): insect which eats and lays its eggs in **dook**.

disgusting fact

Rabbits and baby elephants eat their own poo.

! dunny (noun): Australian slang for toilet.

! dunny budgie (noun): Australian slang for large fly (often found in the **dunny**).

durchfall (noun): German word for diarrhoea.

dur-dur (noun): idiot, a general insult.

durian (noun): tropical fruit which tastes good but smells so disgusting that it is banned in public in some parts of the world.

dust mite (noun): tiny eight-legged bugs that live in the home and eat dead human skin cells.

dut (noun): Vietnamese word for fart.

dweeb (noun): US word for idiot, a general insult.

E
Ebola

! ear candles (verb): see ear wax.

ear wax (noun): moist, yellowy (or grey, dry) substance found in ears to stop dirt from entering the inner ear (also known as ear candles).

! earp (verb): to vomit.

ear probing (verb): disgusting habit of ear wax removal using finger.

earth closet (noun): primitive form of toilet into which earth is shovelled after each use.

ebola (noun): rare disease caused by a virus that turns the internal organs to mush, resulting in painful death.

E

Eew!

eew! (exclamation): expression of disgust.

effluvium (noun): foul smell.

emesis (noun): posh word for vomiting.

emetic (noun): medicine that makes you **chunder** or **squirt**.

entomophagy (noun): the practice of eating insects.

disgusting fact

What we think of as disgusting food depends on where we live. In Asia people think eating cheese is absolutely vile. In Europe and North America, people are revolted by the thought of **entomophagy**.

entrails (noun): internal organs (also known as innards, umbles).

enuresis (noun): posh word for bedwetting.

eructation (noun): posh word for burp.

expectorate (verb): posh word meaning to spit.

eye crust (noun): sticky stuff found in the corner of the eyes on waking up (also known as eye gunk, **sleepies**).

eye gunk (noun): see eye crust.

Faeces

faeces (noun): posh word for poo.

! Farmer Giles (noun): rhyming slang for **piles**.

! fart (noun and verb): to pass **flatus** from the **bahookie**
(see also air biscuit, air buffet, air muffin, air tulip, anal
announcement, anal salute, apple tart, auditorium fart,
backwards burp, baff, bake an air biscuit, bottom bassoon,
bottom blast, bottom burp, bottom trumpet, break wind,
butt burp, buttock bassoon, butt trumpet, church fart,
crack, crepitate, cut a muffin, cut a stinker, cut the cheese,
depth charge, drop one's guts, fice, float an air biscuit,

foist, grime bubble, grunt, guff, gurk, let go a razzo, lay an egg, let off, let off a howler, let off a stinker, let one fly, let one go, let one rip, one-cheek squeak, one-gun salute, open one's lunch, parp, pass gas, pass wind, pocket frog, poot, raspberry tart, rectal rumbling, smelly solo, step on a duck, toot your own horn, trouser cough, trouser trumpet, trump).

disgusting fact

From 1892 to 1914, 'Le Petomane' (French for 'the Fart Maniac') entertained huge audiences in Paris – he would play tunes and blow out candles with his amusing musical behind.

!! **fart-face** (noun): general insult.

!! **fart-head** (noun): general insult.

!! fart-knocker (noun): general insult.

! fat-head (noun): idiot, a general insult.

feculent (adjective): (1) containing poo (2) disgusting or foul.

! feed the fish (verb): to vomit (over the side of a boat or ship).

fester (verb) to rot. The word can also be used as a noun, meaning a pus-filled spot or wound.

fetid (adjective): foul smelling.

! fice (noun): eighteenth century slang word meaning silent fart (also known as church fart, foist).

filth (noun): dirt.

fire ant (noun): small, aggressive ant found mainly in the tropics. Its sting causes an intense burning pain and erupts into an itchy red or purple pustule.

fish eyes (noun): eaten as a delicacy in South East Asia.

! fish-face (noun): general insult (implying ugliness).

flake (noun): idiot, a general insult.

flap-dragon (noun): Elizabethan insult.

flatus (noun): fart gas.

flatulent (adjective): prone to fart.

flea (noun): parasitic insect that lives on the blood of humans and other animals.

fleabag (noun): general insult.

!! fling floor pie (verb): to vomit.

!! float an air biscuit (verb): to fart.

floater (noun): poo still floating in the toilet bowl after flushing.

fly cemetery (noun): bun or biscuit containing currants or raisins.

flying low, you are (phrase): meaning 'your flies are undone'.

! foist (noun): sixteenth-century word meaning silent fart (also known as church fart, fice).

foot-licker (noun): Shakespearean insult (meaning someone who sucks up to other people).

foul (adjective): disgusting.

foul-mouth (noun): someone who uses a lot of disgusting words (also known as muckspout).

frass (noun): posh word for beetle poo.

fribble (noun): idiot, a general insult.

frigate bird (noun): sea bird that forces other birds to ralph and then eats their **boak**.

! frito toes (noun):
US slang for smelly feet.

frowsty (adjective): foul smelling.

fruity (adjective): foul smelling, often applied to **air biscuits**.

fug (noun): unpleasant, stuffy or smelly atmosphere.

fumet (noun): posh word for deer poo.

fundament (noun): bum.

furzen (verb): German word for fart.

fustilarian (noun): Elizabethan insult.

fusty (adjective): stuffy, foul smelling.

! gack (verb): to vomit.

gadzooks! (exclamation): Elizabethan swearword.

gammy (adjective): sick, rotten or septic.

garderobe (noun): Medieval toilet.

gawpus (noun): idiot, a general insult.

gazunder (noun): nineteenth-century word for **chamber pot** (so called because it 'goes under' the bed).

gerber (verb): French word meaning to vomit.

germ (noun): tiny organism that causes disease.

! gilbert (noun): small bogey.

ghastly (adjective): horrible.

ghoul (noun): ghost; especially one that eats dead bodies in graveyards in the dead of night.

glaikit (adjective): Scottish slang for stupid.

! gob (noun and verb): a globule of spit, or to spit (also known as gollier, goober, gozz, quag).

! gobdaw (noun): Irish slang for idiot, a general insult.

göbeln (verb): German word for vomit.

! go commando (verb): to wear trousers but no underpants.

! gollier (noun): Irish slang for especially big **goober**.

gom/gombeen (noun): Irish slang for idiot, a general insult.

disgusting fact

Camels spit regurgitated food at things or people they don't like.

gompf stick (noun): Medieval scraper used instead of toilet paper.

gong farmer (noun): person who cleaned a Medieval castle toilet.

! goober (noun): a globule of spit, or gob.

goop (noun): anything runny, sticky and (usually) unpleasant.

Gorgon (noun): three **buttly** ugly sisters with snakes for hair from Greek mythology. Anyone who looked at them was turned to stone by their extreme repulsiveness.

! gorm (noun): idiot, a general insult.

! gozz (noun and verb): spit.

‼ greenie (noun): particularly nasty gob (one containing phlegm).

grime (noun): dirt.

‼ grime bubble (noun): fart.

grimy (adjective): dirty.

grody (adjective): North American slang for disgusting (also known as cruddy).

gross (adjective): disgusting.

grot (noun): something unpleasant or dirty.

grotty (adjective): dirty or unpleasant, **manky**.

grubby (adjective): dirty.

gruesome (adjective): horrible, revolting.

grufted (adjective): dirty.

grunge (noun): dirt (especially of the messy, sticky variety), **guck**.

grungy (adjective): dirty, **cruddy**.

! **grunt** (noun and verb): fart.

guano (noun): the poo of sea birds.

! **guck** (noun): anything slimy, sticky and unpleasant (such as **beakie**).

gudgeon (noun): Elizabethan word meaning idiot, a general insult.

! **guff** (noun and verb): (1) fart (2) can also be used to mean nonsense in the phrase: 'you're talking a lot of old guff'.

gump (noun): eighteenth-century word meaning fool, a general insult.

gunge (noun): something dirty, sticky and disgusting (also known as guck).

gunk (noun): something dirty, sticky and disgusting (such as **toe jam**).

!! gurk (noun and verb): fart.

Haggis

H

haggis (noun): Scottish dish made from the **umbles** of a sheep, mixed with oatmeal and boiled inside the sheep's stomach.

hakarl (noun): Icelandic dish made from shark meat which has been buried and left to putrefy for several months, then dried and eaten.

halfwit (noun): idiot, a general insult.

halitosis (noun): posh word for bad breath.

head (noun): ship toilet.

headcase (noun): crazed person, a general insult.

head cheese (noun): jelly-like substance produced by boiling animal heads (see also brawn).

head louse (noun): tiny louse which lives and feeds on the blood from the human head (plural: head lice).

! **heave** (verb): to vomit.

!! **heave one's cookies** (verb): to vomit.

hindquarters (noun): bum.

‼ honk (verb): to vomit.

hookworm (noun): parasitic worm which lives by attaching itself to the human intestine.

‼ hork (verb): to vomit.

horse apple (noun): piece of horse dung (also known as horse biscuit, horse dumpling, road apple).

horse biscuit (noun): see horse apple.

horse dumpling (noun): see horse apple.

‼ huey (verb): to vomit.

hum (noun and verb): bad smell.

humming (adjective): smelly or disgusting.

humgruffin (noun): nineteenth-century word meaning repulsive person, a general insult.

!! hurl (verb): to vomit.

hyperhidrosis (noun): posh word for excessive sweating.

Ick!

Ick! (exclamation): expression of disgust.

icky (adjective): disgusting.

indole (noun): one of the two chemicals (along with **skatole**) that causes poo (and farts) to smell.

ineffables (noun): nineteenth-century word for trousers.

inexpressibles (noun): nineteenth-century word for trousers.

innards (noun): internal organs (see also **entrails**).

itch mite (noun): tiny parasite that burrows underneath the skin, causing **scabies**.

disgusting fact

It is thought that eating meat produces the smelliest farts of all.

Jacksie

J

!! **jacksie** (noun): British slang for bum.

jacks (noun): Irish word for toilet.

jakes (noun): toilet.

jamba (noun): Swahili word for fart (also known as shuzi).

jellied eels (noun): traditional dish served in the East End of London consisting of cold, cooked eels in gelatine.

jerk (noun): unpleasant or foolish person, a general insult.

jerry-come-tumble (noun): nineteenth-century word for poo.

jerry-go-nimble (noun): nineteenth-century word for diarrhoea.

jimmy riddle (noun): rhyming slang for piddle.

job (noun): poo.

jobberknowl (noun): sixteenth-century word meaning idiot, a general insult.

jobby (noun): poo.

john (noun): US word for toilet.

Kaka

kaka (noun): German and Greek word for poo.

kaynard (noun): lazy coward, a general insult.

!! keech (noun): Scottish word meaning poo (note that the 'ch' is pronounced as in the word 'loch').

! keister (noun): North American word for bum.

khazi (noun): toilet.

killer bees (noun): Africanised honey bees, given the name killer bees because they can viciously attack people or animals who stray into their territory, inflicting multiple stings which can be fatal.

kissing bug (noun): see assassin bug.

!! **kiss the porcelain god** (verb): to vomit.

klo (noun): German word for toilet.

klutz (noun): US word for clumsy person, a general insult.

knickers (noun): underpants (usually referring to girl's or women's underwear).

knucklehead (noun): idiot, a general insult.

knuckle-sandwich (noun): fierce punch in the mouth.

kübeln (verb): German word for vomit (also known as reihern).

lack-linen (noun): Shakespearean insult.

lamebrain (noun): fool, a general insult.

‼ lateral cookie toss (noun): vomit.

latrine (noun): toilet.

‼ launch lunch (verb): to vomit.

lavatory (noun): posh word for toilet.

lavvy (noun): toilet.

laxative (noun): medicine that makes you poo.

lay an egg (verb): to fart.

leech (noun): parasitic worm, found in most parts of the world, that feeds on blood. In the past, leeches were used by doctors to 'bleed' patients. Today, doctors use them to prevent blood from clotting.

disgusting fact

A leech can gorge itself on up to five times its own body weight in blood.

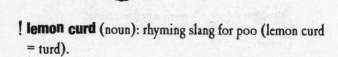

! lemon curd (noun): rhyming slang for poo (lemon curd = turd).

lesses (noun): posh word for the poo of a bear, wolf, or boar.

! let go a razzo (verb): nineteenth-century slang for fart.

!! let off (noun and verb): fart.

!! let off a howler (verb): to fart.

!! let off a stinker (verb): to fart.

!! let one fly (verb): to fart.

!! let one go (verb): to fart.

!! let one rip (verb): to fart.

! lights are on but there's no one at home, the (phrase): expression meaning that while someone may appear perfectly normal, in fact they are very stupid (see also wheel's turning but the hamster's dead, the).

!! liquid laugh (noun): Australian slang for vomit.

!! liquid scream (noun): Australian slang for vomit.

little boys'/little girls' room (noun): toilet.

living dead (noun): dead body supposed to have been brought back to life in order to do the bidding of a supernatural force (also known as undead, zombie).

loathsome (adjective): hateful, horrible, disgusting.

loffare (verb): Italian word meaning to fart (noun = loffa), (also known as **scorreggiare**).

! log (noun): poo.

long drop (noun): a hole-in-the-ground toilet.

loo (noun): toilet.

! look for O'Rourke (verb): to vomit.

loupin' (adjective): disgusting (originally Scottish).

lout (noun): a rough, ignorant person (also known as oik, yob).

!! lose your cookies (verb): to vomit.

!! lose your lunch (verb): to vomit.

louse (noun): small parasitic insect which lives on humans and animals (plural: lice). May also be used as a general insult.

louse fly (noun): bloodsucking fly which spends most of its life on an individual animal.

lousy (adjective): (1) infested with lice (2) very bad, or useless.

lulu (noun): German word for pee.

lummox (noun): clumsy fool, a general insult.

lunkhead (noun): idiot, a general insult.

maggot (noun): wormlike larva of an insect.

maggot-brained (adjective): idiotic, a general insult.

maggot cheese (noun): special cheese made in Sardinia. Sheep's cheese is left out in the sun until maggots hatch out in it, then the cheese is eaten, complete with live maggots.

maggot-pie (noun): Shakespearean insult.

! make room for seconds (verb): to vomit.

malodorous (adjective): foul smelling.

malt worm (noun): Elizabethan insult (a malt worm is a weevil that infests alcohol).

mange (noun): skin disease caused by mites, found in animals and sometimes in humans.

mangy (adjective): (1) having **mange** (2) in bad condition.

manky (adjective): dirty, **cruddy**.

manure (noun): dung.

mear (verb): Spanish word for pee.

meatbrain (noun): idiot, a general insult.

Medusa (noun): the name of the most famous **Gorgon**.

! melvin (noun): the condition of having one's trousers or underpants caught between the buttocks (also known as wedgie).

mephitic (adjective): foul smelling — of **bromhidrosis**, for example.

micturate (verb): posh word meaning to pee.

midden (noun): dung- or rubbish-heap.

!! minger (noun): very unpleasant or unattractive person or thing (originally Scottish).

mingin' (adjective): disgusting or smelly - originally Scottish, (see also bowffin').

mist (noun): German word for poo.

mite (noun): tiny eight-legged parasitic creature which infests animals and humans.

disgusting fact

Microscopic eight-legged mites live in your eyelashes.

Mongolian death worm: from Mongolian folklore. A metre-long, highly aggressive red worm, said to kill people by spraying them with deadly acid. Its local name is **Allghoi Khorkhoi**.

monkey-brains (noun): idiot, a general insult.

!! Montezuma's revenge (noun): diarrhoea (particularly when on holiday abroad).

! moon (verb): to display one's bum.

! mork (noun): general insult (a cross between a **moron** and a **dork**).

! moron (noun): idiot, a general insult.

mould (noun): furry growth (a type of fungus) that grows on rotting organic matter.

muck (noun): dirt or poo.

muckspout (noun): someone who uses a lot of disgusting words (also known as foul-mouth).

mucus (noun): runny, slimy substance produced by the nose, throat and lungs.

mullock (noun): nineteenth-century word for useless person, a general insult.

! multicoloured yawn (noun): vomit.

mundungus (adjective): eighteenth-century word for foul smelling.

mutes (noun): posh word for the poo of a hawk.

myxa (noun): Greek word for snot.

disgusting fact

Snot from a sneeze can travel up to 3.5 metres.

nail-biting (noun): disgusting habit of biting one's fingernails (and in extreme cases toenails).

nappy (adjective): disgusting (mainly US).

nausea (noun): the feeling of being about to **chunder**.

nauseating (adjective): causing the feeling of being about to **chunder**.

nauseous (adjective): feeling as though one is about to **chunder**.

necessaries, the (noun): nineteenth-century word for toilet.

necessary house (noun): nineteenth-century word for toilet.

ned (noun): Irish slang for poo.

nelly (noun): general insult.

Nematode worm (noun): type of worm that can infest the human digestive system.

nero (noun): Greek word for pee.

nettie (noun): toilet (originally from Northern England).

nidorous (adjective): smelling strongly of burned or rotting animal meat or dung.

niff (noun and verb): bad smell.

night soil (noun): poo (produced at night).

nit (noun): see head louse.

noisome (adjective): disgusting, foul-smelling.

nose-picking (noun and verb): the disgusting habit of removing bogies from the nose using a finger.

! number one (noun): pee.

! number two (noun): poo.

numptie (noun): idiot, a general insult (originally Scottish).

obraderas (noun): Spanish word for diarrhoea.

odour (noun): smell, normally used to describe an unpleasant smell.

offal (noun): animal innards used as food.

oik (noun): a rough, ignorant person (also known as lout, yob).

onara (noun): Japanese word for fart.

onychophagia (noun): posh word for nail-biting.

disgusting fact

The world record for long fingernails is held by Shridhar Chillal: the nails on his left hand were measured at over 6 metres long altogether. He hadn't cut them for 43 years.

‼ one-cheek squeak (noun): fart.

‼ one-gun salute (noun): fart.

open one's lunch (verb): Australian word meaning to fart.

ordure (noun): poo.

outhouse (noun): outside toilet.

Padhh

padhh (noun): Hindi word for fart.

palace (noun): toilet.

palmar hyperhidrosis (noun): posh word for unusually sweaty palms.

! palooka (noun): idiot, a general insult.

pan (noun): toilet.

pants (noun): (1) underwear, knickers (2) rubbish or useless.

parasite (noun): creature or plant that lives inside or on another creature, from which the parasite gets its food, usually at the expense (or even death) of the host creature.

!! park a leopard (verb): to vomit.

parking place (noun): bum.

!! park one's breakfast (verb): to vomit.

! parp (noun and verb): fart.

pass gas (verb): to fart.

pass water (verb): to pee.

pass wind (verb): to fart.

‼ Patagonian pasodoble (noun): diarrhoea (particularly when on holiday abroad).

‼ pavement pizza (noun): heap of vomit found in the street.

pay a visit (verb): to go to the toilet.

pedo (noun): Spanish word for fart.

pee (noun and verb): urine (also known as jimmy riddle, micturate, number one, pass water, piddle, pump ship, spend a penny, take a leak, tiddle, tinkle, urine, water the garden, water the tomatoes, wazz, whizz, widdle.)

peidar (verb): Portuguese word for fart.

pen and ink (noun and verb): rhyming slang for stink.

péter (verb): French word for fart.

disgusting fact

Some animals have especially disgusting toilet habits: flamingoes pee down their legs to cool down and bushbabies pee on their hands to mark their scent.

phlegm (noun): slimy, thick, often greenish substance produced in the throat.

piddle (noun and verb): pee.

piesen (verb): Dutch word for pee.

pig's trotters (noun): dish consisting of a pig's hind feet, either pickled or boiled and served either hot or cold, eaten in many parts of the world (also known as crubeen).

piles (noun): a distressing and unpleasant condition of the fundament.

Pillock

pillock (noun): idiot, a general insult.

pimple (noun): spot, zit.

pinkein (verb): German word for pee.

pinworm (noun): parasitic worm that infests humans and causes (among other things) an itchy **keister**.

pipi (noun): French, Italian and Portuguese word for pee.

piranha fish (noun): fish found in the rivers of South America. The fish have a ferocious reputation: shoals of piranha can attack and kill large animals (such as humans).

place of easement (noun): nineteenth-century word for toilet.

plague (noun): a deadly contagious disease (see also bubonic plague).

plank (noun): idiot, a general insult.

plantar hyperhidrosis (noun): posh word for unusually sweaty feet.

plaque (noun): disgusting layer of bacteria and food that builds up on teeth.

! **plock** (noun): poo.

plonker (noun): idiot, a general insult.

plook (noun): Scottish word for zit (also known as pluke).

! **plop** (noun): poo.

plug ugly (adjective): very ugly.

pluke (noun): see plook.

!! pocket frog (noun): fart.

pockmark (noun): small scar left by a spot.

pod (noun): Bengali word for bum.

pogue ma hone (phrase): Irish Gaelic for 'kiss my bum'.

poison arrow frog (noun): small, brightly coloured frog found in the rainforests of South America. The frog produces poison through its **mucus**-covered skin, only 2 micrograms of which is enough to kill an adult human (one frog has about 200 micrograms of poison in its body). The Choco tribe of Indians uses poison from the frogs for their arrows and darts.

polyhidrosis (noun): posh word for excessive sweating.

pong (noun and verb): bad smell, **niff**.

ponk (noun and verb): bad smell, **hum**.

poo (noun): dung (see also bondi cigar, brown-eyed mullet, brown trout, cack, crap, defecate, doo-doo, dook, droppings, dump, faeces, floater, jerry-come-tumble, job, jobby, keech, lemon curd, log, muck, ned, night soil, number two, plock, plop, poop, Richard the Third, scat, stool, turd, whoopsie.)

poon (noun): Urdu word for fart.

disgusting fact

The Tokyo Science Museum in Japan exhibited a collection of 78 different types of human and animal **dung**.

poop (noun): poo.

pooper-scooper (noun): small shovel used for removing dog poo from parks and pavements (mainly used in the US).

poop-head (noun): idiot, a general insult.

poop-stick (noun): unpleasant person, a general insult.

poot (noun and verb): fart.

porda (noun) Greek word for fart.

Portuguese man-of-war (noun): deadly, jellyfish-like sea creature. The colourful (often blue) floating animal has long tentacles trailing beneath it which sting painfully and can be fatal. Also known in Australia as a bluebottle or bluey.

posterior (noun): bum.

potato-head (noun): idiot, a general insult.

potty (noun): (1) chamber pot (2) Urdu word for poo (3) toilet used by young children.

powder one's nose (verb): to go to the toilet.

powder room (noun): toilet.

powsodie (noun): whole sheep's head, complete with brains, cooked and served in broth, traditional in Scotland.

pox (noun): a viral disease which causes a rash of pustules, such as chicken pox.

poxy (adjective): (1) suffering from pox, or spotty. (2) unpleasant, **manky**.

prannet (noun): idiot, a general insult.

pray to the porcelain god (verb): to vomit.

prd (noun): Czech word for fart.

prdel (noun): Czech word for bum.

privy (noun): toilet (probably an outside toilet).

projectile vomit (noun and verb): vomit propelled with great force, common in babies.

prout (noun): French word for fart.

public convenience (noun): public toilet.

puffoon (noun): bad smell – of a **pocket frog**, for example.

puke (noun and verb): vomit.

puky (adjective): sick-making or disgusting.

pum (noun): Portuguese word for fart.

! pump bilge (verb): to vomit.

pumpion (noun): Shakespearean insult.

! pump ship (verb): to pee.

pus (noun): thick yellowish substance found in pimples or wounds, made up of bacteria, **sebum** and dead tissue.

pustule (noun): spot or pimple containing pus.

putrefaction (noun): rot, decomposition; often the cause of an offensive smell.

putrefy (verb): to rot.

putrid (adjective): rotting and foul-smelling.

puttock (noun): Shakespearean insult.

! **puzzlegut** (noun): early twentieth-century insult meaning large-stomached.

pyroflatulate (verb): to light one's farts.

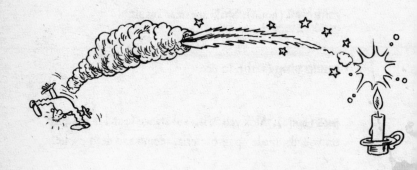

!! quag (noun): **phlegmy** snot globule (see also gob).

quakebuttock (noun): eighteenth-century insult meaning large-bottomed.

quease (verb): to vomit.

queasy (adjective): **nauseous**.

rag and bone (noun): rhyming slang for toilet (rag and bone = throne).

!! ralph (verb): to vomit.

rancid (adjective): smelling or tasting disgusting; particularly used of food that has gone bad.

!! Rangoon runs (noun): diarrhoea (particularly when on holiday abroad).

rank (adjective): disgusting, foul-smelling.

rännskita (noun): Swedish word for diarrhoea.

rapscallion (noun): villainous person, a general insult from the word 'rascallion' originally used in the seventeenth-century.

! raspberry tart (noun): rhyming slang for fart. To 'blow raspberries' means to make a farting noise.

disgusting fact

Cows fart about 300 times a day – that's 450 litres of wind.

ratbag (noun): unpleasant person, a general insult.

rat-face (noun): general insult.

rear (noun): bum.

rear end (noun): bum.

!! rectal rumbling (noun): fart.

! red hots (noun): diarrhoea (rhyming slang for **trots**).

reechy (adjective): filthy.

reek (verb): to stink.

regurgitate (verb): to bring up swallowed food.

reihern (verb): German word for vomit (also known as kubeln).

repulsive (adjective): disgusting.

restroom (noun): toilet (mainly US).

retch (verb): to vomit.

!! return the tripe (verb): to vomit.

revolting (adjective): disgusting.

rhinorrhoea (noun): posh word for snotty nose.

rhinotillexomania (noun) posh word for nose-picking.

‼ Richard the Third (noun): rhyming slang for poo (Richard the Third = turd).

road apples (noun): horse droppings.

roasted ants (noun): dish eaten in South America.

roasted guinea-pig (noun): dish eaten in Peru.

robin's eye (noun): nineteenth-century slang for a scab or sore.

rogue with one ear (noun): seventeenth-century slang for a chamber pot.

rôpe pa elgen (phrase): Norwegian phrase meaning to vomit (literally 'to call the moose').

R

Rope pa elgen

rot (verb): to decay.

rotten (adjective): decayed.

rotz (noun): German word for snot.

rump (noun): bum.

runny tummy (noun): diarrhoea.

! runs, the (noun): diarrhoea.

!! rusty water (noun): diarrhoea.

S

sago worms (noun): the larvae of beetles, which are eaten either raw, roasted, fried or stewed in many parts of Asia.

saliva (noun): clear liquid produced in the mouth that begins the process of food digestion (also known as spit or spittle).

scab (noun): the crust of hardened pus and blood that forms on a wound or sore.

scabby (adjective): having lots of scabs. Can also be used to describe anything unpleasant or **scuzzy**.

scabies (noun): contagious, itchy skin condition caused by itch mites.

scat (noun): poo.

scatological (adjective): having to do with poo.

scatology (noun): the study of poo (also known as **coprology**).

scent bottle (noun): nineteenth-century word for toilet.

schleim (noun): German word for snot.

scitte (noun): Old English word for diarrhoea.

scomm (noun): buffoon, a general insult.

scorreggiare (verb): Italian word for fart (also known as loffare).

scraping castle (noun): nineteenth-century word for toilet.

scroyle (noun): villain, a general insult.

scum (noun): (1) any foam or froth that floats on the surface of liquid (2) anything worthless, including people thought to be worthless.

! scumbag (noun): general insult containing the suggestion that the person so described is also a **soap dodger** or **dirt surfer**.

scumber (noun): scientific word for dog poo.

scummy (adjective): dirty, manky.

!! scutters, the (noun): Irish slang for diarrhoea.

scuzzy (adjective): dirty or disgusting.

seal-flipper pie (noun): dish eaten in parts of Canada.

sea wasp (noun): a type of jellyfish, also known as a box jellyfish, common off the coast of Northern Australia. It has metres of stinging tentacles which, if they come into contact with human skin, result in excruciating pain and are usually fatal.

seborrheic dermatitis (noun): posh word for dandruff.

seborrhoea (noun): excessive production of **sebum**, which often resullts in **plooks**.

sebum (noun): oily substance produced by the sebaceous glands on the skin.

septic tank (noun): tank containing sewage.

sewage (noun): human and industrial waste carried by sewers.

disgusting fact

Some people think drinking urine is good for you. The ancient Chinese used it as a cure for gum disease and a French doctor was recommending it as a mouthwash in the 18th century. The Ancient Romans left large containers in the street to collect the pee of passers-by: they used it to clean laundry.

sewer (noun): channel or pipe which carries away waste from **cludgies** and drains.

shoo-shoo (noun): Urdu word for urine (also known as cheey-cheey).

!! **shoot one's cookies** (verb): to vomit.

!! **shout at one's shoes** (verb): to vomit.

shreddies (noun): underpants.

shuzi (noun): Swahili word for fart (also known as jamba).

sick (noun): vomit.

sickening (adjective): disgusting, **nauseating**.

!! **sing a rainbow** (verb): to vomit.

sit-me-down (noun): nineteenth-century word for bum.

sit-upon (noun): nineteenth-century word for bum.

sitting room (noun): nineteenth-century word for bum.

skatole (noun): one of the two chemicals (along with indole) which causes poo (and farts) to smell.

disgusting fact

Farts are mostly made up of the gas nitrogen. Some foods combine in the gut to make hydrogen sulphide, which is why some farts smell like rotten eggs.

skellum (noun): seventeenth-century word meaning scoundrel, a general insult.

skit (noun): Swedish word for poo.

!! skitters (noun): diarrhoea.

skrungy (adjective): disgusting.

skunk (noun): small animal found in North America which sprays a disgustingly foul smelling liquid from a gland near its **bahookie**.

slaver (verb): to let saliva run from the mouth (see also dribble).

sleepies (noun): sticky stuff found in the corner of the eyes on waking up (also known as eye crust, eye gunk).

slime (noun): any unpleasant gluey substance.

slimebag (noun): unpleasant person, a general insult.

Snot

slimeball (noun): unpleasant person, a general insult.

slimebucket (noun): unpleasant person, a general insult.

! slummock (noun): lazy, good-for-nothing person.

smallest room (noun): toilet.

smellfungus (noun): eighteenth-century insult meaning grumbling, miserable person.

!! smelly solo (noun): fart.

snig/sniggy (noun): bogey.

snorbobba (noun): Swedish word for snot.

snot (noun): mucus found in the **snotter** (see also bat-in-a-cave, blow snot rockets, bogey, booger, bushman's hanky, bush oyster, candlestick, gilbert, rhinorrhoea, snig, sniggy).

disgusting fact

Ancient Greek doctor Hippocrates, thought it was a good idea to smell and taste patients' snot, pee and earwax.

snot-box (noun): nineteenth-century word for nose.

snot-horn (noun): eighteenth-century word for nose.

snot rag (noun): handkerchief.

snotter (noun): nineteenth-century word for nose.

soap dodger (noun): a dirty or unhygienic person (also known as dirt surfer).

soldier ants (noun): rhyming slang for pants.

! sour-apple quickstep (noun): diarrhoea.

souse-crown (noun): seventeenth-century word meaning idiot.

spend a penny (verb): to pee.

! spew (noun and verb): vomit.

!! spew spuds (verb): to vomit.

spit (noun and verb): saliva, or to eject saliva.

!! spit bits (verb): to vomit.

spittle (noun): saliva.

spittoon (noun): container for spitting into (also known as cuspidor).

spit up (verb): to vomit (mainly US).

‼ **split pea stew** (noun): vomit.

spot (noun): **pustule** (see also abscess, boil, carbunkle, chorb, fester, pimple, pustule, plook, wen, whitehead, zit).

spraint (noun): posh word for otter poo.

sputum (noun): saliva, mucus or phlegm spat out of the mouth.

‼ **squirt** (verb): to pass diarrhoea.

!! squirts, the (noun): diarrhoea.

!! squits, the (noun): diarrhoea.

!! squitters, the (noun): diarrhoea

stench (noun): very bad smell, **puffoon**.

step on a duck (verb): to fart.

stink (noun and verb): bad smell, **hum**.

stink bomb (noun): glass container which, when smashed, releases a terrible **stench**.

stinkeroo (noun): something or someone disgusting.

! stinkheads (noun): Alaskan dish of fish heads buried for several months and then eaten.

stinkpot (noun): unpleasant person (possibly a **dirt surfer**), a general insult.

!! stool (noun): posh word for a piece of poo.

study at the library (verb): to go to the toilet.

stumblebum (noun): idiot, a general insult.

suppurate (verb): to discharge pus.

su-su (noun): Hindi word for pee.

! swap spit (verb): to kiss.

sweat (noun and verb): liquid produced by glands all over the skin, which will become smelly over time and may result in body odour.

swounds! (exclamation): Elizabethan swear word.

disgusting fact

Only teenagers and adults have smelly sweat. Until you're about twelve, the glands that produce pongy sweat aren't active.

Tail

T

tail (noun): bum.

! take a leak (verb): to pee.

!! talk to Ralph on the big white telephone (verb): to vomit.

Tamandua anteater
(noun): particular type of
anteater found in South
America and known as 'the
stinker of the forest'
because of its foul stench.

tapeworm (noun): parasitic worm which lives in animal and human intestines. One type of tapeworm can reach up to 9 metres in length and live for many years.

tatu (noun): Portuguese word for snot.

!! **technicolour yawn** (noun): vomit.

throne (noun): toilet.

!! **throw one's cookies** (verb): to vomit.

throw up (verb): to vomit.

thunderbox (noun): toilet.

!! **thunderchunder** (noun and verb): vomit.

thundermug (noun): chamber pot.

thunderpot (noun): chamber pot.

tick (noun): tiny eight-legged parasite which attaches itself to animals and humans and feeds on their blood.

tiddle (noun and verb): pee.

tinkle (noun and verb): pee.

Titan Arum (noun): see corpse flower.

! toe jam (noun): grimy, sticky bits found between the toes (see also **beakie**) – evidence of being a **soap dodger**.

toe rag (noun): villain, a general insult.

disgusting fact

Thomas Crapper didn't invent the toilet, but he did design and make toilets in the 19th century.

toilet (noun): essential piece of plumbing equipment which collects and disposes of pee and **ordure** (see also bathroom, bean jacks, biffy, bog, bog house, can, cloakroom, closet of ease, cludgie, comfort station, dunny, earth closet, garderobe, head, jacks, jakes, john, khazi, latrine, lavatory, lavvy, little boys'/girls' room, long drop, loo, the necessaries, necessary house, nettie, outhouse, palace, place of easement, powder room, privy, public convenience, rag and bone, restroom, scent bottle, scraping castle, smallest room, throne, thunderbox, washroom, water closet, W.C.)

tokhes (noun): Yiddish word for bum.

tom tug (noun): nineteenth-century slang for **bedbug** (also known as crimson rambler).

! toosh (noun): bum.

! tooshie (noun): bum.

!! toot your own horn (verb): to fart.

!! toss a tiger (verb): to vomit.

!! toss (one's) cookies (verb): to vomit.

tragomaschalia (noun): posh word for smelly armpits.

tripe (noun): different types of tripe are made from three of a cow's four stomachs. It is eaten in many parts of the world, particularly Europe.

trollies (noun): underpants.

!! trots, the (noun): diarrhoea.

!!! trouser chilli (noun): diarrhoea.

‼ trouser cough (noun): fart.

‼ trouser trumpet (noun): fart.

❗ trump (noun and verb): fart.

tuckus (noun): bum.

disgusting fact

Victorian lecturer William Buckland
tried many strange and disgusting
foods, including bluebottles, an
elephant's trunk and the
mummified heart of Louis XIV.

Turd

!! turd (noun): poo.

twerp (noun): idiot, a general insult.

twit (noun): idiot, a general insult.

?!

TWIT, TWIT TWERP!

ulcer (noun): open sore.

umbles (noun): internal organs (also known as entrails, innards).

Uncle Dick (noun): rhyming slang for sick.

undead (noun and adjective): dead body supposed to have been brought back to life in order to do the bidding of a supernatural force (also known as living dead, zombie).

undercrackers (noun): underpants.

underkecks (noun): underpants.

‼ undy-grundy (noun): Irish word for **wedgie**.

unmentionables (noun): nineteenth-century word for trousers.

untalkaboutables (noun): nineteenth-century word for trousers.

disgusting fact

In the 19th century people were disgusted by almost everything. To protect sensitive ears from words they thought of as disgusting, the Victorians thought up euphemisms – words or phrases used as more polite substitutes for the offending words.

unutterables (noun): nineteenth-century word for trousers.

unwhisperables (noun): nineteenth-century word for trousers.

! upchuck (noun and verb): vomit.

urine (noun): posh word for pee.

urky-purky (adjective): disgusting.

Vampire

V

vampire (noun): dead body supposed to come to life at night and suck the blood of living human beings.

verruca (noun): contagious wart on the sole of the foot.

verstopfung (noun): German word for constipation.

vile (adjective): disgusting.

violet cart (noun): cart that came to take away the contents of **chamber pots** and **earth closets** in the nineteenth-century.

viscera (noun): large internal organs.

‼ visible burp (noun): vomit.

visit Sir Harry (verb): nineteenth-century word meaning to go to the toilet.

visit the smallest room (verb): to go to the toilet.

vomit (noun and verb): partially digested food that makes a reappearance via the mouth when a person is ill (see also air the diced carrots, barf, bark at ants, bark carrots, blow beets, blow breakfast, blow chunks, blow foam, blow (one's) lunch, boak, bowff, burp borscht, call Huey, chew the cheese, chuck up, chunder, chunderspew, chunk (one's) cookies, chunk (one's) lunch, curl and hurl, decorate the pavement, deliver pavement pizza, disgorge, do a cat, drive the porcelain bus, earp, feed the fish, fling

floor pie, floor pie, gack, heave, heave (one's) cookies, honk, hork, huey, hurl, kiss the porcelain god, lateral cookie toss, launch lunch, liquid laugh, liquid scream, look for O'Rourke, lose (one's) cookies, lose (one's) lunch, make room for seconds, multicoloured yawn, park a leopard, park (one's) breakfast, pavement pizza, pray to the porcelain god, puke, pump bilge, quease, ralph, retch, return the tripe, shoot (one's) cookies, shout at (one's) shoes, sick, sing a rainbow, spew, spew spuds, spit bits, spit up, split pea stew, talk to ralph, technicolour yawn, throw (one's) cookies, throw up, thunderchunder, toss (one's) cookies, toss a tiger, upchuck, visible burp, vomit up (one's) toenails, vurp, woof, woof (one's) cookies, worship at the porcelain altar, yack, yark, yawn, yodel, yodel yoghurt, york, yuck up.)

vomitorium

(noun): in Ancient Rome, a room where diners could go and **spew spuds** in order to make room for more food.

vomitous (adjective): nauseating.

vomitrocious (adjective): absolutely disgusting (a combination of the words vomit and atrocious).

vomit up (one's) toenails (verb): to **york** especially forcefully, producing an unusually large amount of **chunder**.

vulgar (adjective): rude, prone to use of disgusting words and references to bodily functions.

!!! vurp (noun): a burp that results in a tiny amount of vomit.

Wally

wally (noun): idiot, a general insult.

wart (noun): a hardened growth on the skin.

washroom (noun): toilet.

water bug (noun): tropical insect that can fly and swim. It can inflict a nasty stab to humans with its sharp beak, which it uses to suck out the bodily fluids of its prey (mainly tadpoles and other insects). Water bugs are eaten as a delicacy in many parts of Asia.

water closet (noun): toilet.

water the garden (verb): to pee.

water the tomatoes (verb): to pee.

‼ wazz (noun and verb): pee.

❗ wazzock (noun): idiot, a general insult.

❗ wazzoo (noun): US word for bum.

W.C. (noun): abbreviation of **water closet**.

‼ wedgie (noun): the act of pulling someone's underpants forcefully upwards by the waistband, resulting in an extreme **melvin** (see also atomic wedgie, undy-grundy).

wembley (noun): a patch of pee visible on clothing following a trip to the **biffy**.

wen (noun): **pus**-filled swelling on skin, **boil**.

wendigo (noun): North American Indian evil spirit that eats human flesh and turns its victims into man-eating monsters.

! wheel's still turning but the hamster's dead, the (phrase): meaning that while someone may appear perfectly normal, in fact they are very stupid (see also lights are on but there's nobody at home, the).

whiffy (adjective): bad smelling, of a **trouser cough**, for example.

whitehead (noun): spot with white pustular top.

white pudding (noun): sausage skin stuffed with beef fat and oatmeal, popular in Scotland.

! whiz (noun): pee.

whoopsie (noun): poo.

widdle (noun and verb): pee.

! wildies, the (noun): diarrhoea.

wimp (noun): weak or ineffectual person, a general insult.

witchety grub (noun): fat, worm-like insect larva eaten in Australia, either alive, roasted or fried.

!! woof (verb): to vomit.

!! woof one's cookies (verb): to vomit.

workman's bum (noun): see builder's bum.

! worship at the porcelain altar (verb): to vomit.

! wuss (noun): weak, pathetic person, a general insult.

Y

!! yack (verb): to vomit.

yacky (adjective): disgusting.

!! yark (verb): to vomit.

! yawn (verb): to vomit.

Y-fronts (noun): particularly unattractive type of underpants worn by boys or men.

yob (noun): a rough, ignorant person (also known as lout).

Yodel

! yodel (verb): to vomit.

!! yodel yoghurt (verb): to vomit.

!! york (verb): to vomit.

!! yuck up (verb): to vomit.

yucky (adjective): disgusting.

zit (noun): spot, or **chorb**.

!! zit-zapper (noun): someone with a lot of **plooks**.

zombie (noun): dead body supposed to have been brought back to life in order to do the bidding of a supernatural force (also known as living dead, undead).

zoom-in (noun): an unwanted and unexpected kiss.

zoonosis (noun): any disease that can be spread to humans by animals.

Zorba

zorba (verb): rhyming slang for pee. Zorba the Greek =
take a leak (*Zorba the Greek* is the title of a famous
novel by author Nikos Kazantakis).

zounds! (exclamation): Elizabethan swearword.